Sustainability: Save our Planet and Future Lives

Author: NHIMSK

Abstract: "Sustainability: Nurturing Our Planet for Future Generations" is a comprehensive book that explores the concept of sustainability and its significance in creating a prosperous and harmonious future.

It covers various dimensions of sustainability, including climate change, resource conservation, circular economy, biodiversity, agriculture, waste management, social equity, transportation, and urbanization. The book examines the consequences of unsustainable practices, offers practical solutions, and highlights the need for action. Drawing on research, case studies, and expert insights, it provides a roadmap for individuals, organizations, and policymakers to embrace sustainable practices and build a resilient and equitable world.

This accessible resource serves as a valuable guide for students, professionals, and anyone interested in sustainability and safeguarding the planet for future generations.

Copyright Warning

Disclaimer

The information contained in this book is provided for general informational purposes only. While every effort has been made to ensure the accuracy and completeness of the content, the author and publisher make no representations or warranties of any kind, express or implied, about the suitability, reliability, or availability of the information, products, services, or related graphics contained in this book for any purpose. The content of this book is not intended to be a substitute for professional advice or guidance, and readers are encouraged to seek the assistance of qualified professionals in applying the concepts and ideas discussed. The author and publisher disclaim any liability for any loss or damage arising from the reliance on the information provided in this book or from any actions taken based on the content. The inclusion of any external links or references does not imply endorsement or recommendation by the author and publisher. The views expressed in this book are solely those of the author and do not necessarily reflect the views of the publisher or any affiliated individuals or organizations.

Table of Contents

Sustainability: Save our Planet and Future Lives

Sustainability encompasses a wide range of important topics that aim to address and mitigate environmental, social, and economic challenges. Here are some key topics within the realm of sustainability:

Climate Change: Climate change refers to long-term shifts in temperature patterns and weather conditions, largely attributed to human activities such as burning fossil fuels and deforestation. Addressing climate change involves reducing greenhouse gas emissions, transitioning to renewable energy sources, and implementing adaptation strategies.

Renewable Energy: Transitioning to renewables is vital in reducing emissions and combating climate change. Solar, wind, hydro, geothermal, and bioenergy offer sustainable solutions. Investing in renewable infrastructure is key for a greener future.

Resource Conservation: Sustainable resource management responsibly uses natural resources, promotes efficiency, recycling, and conservation to ensure their long-term availability for a greener future.

Circular Economy: The concept of a circular economy aims to minimize waste and maximize resource efficiency. It involves designing products for durability, reusing and recycling materials, and adopting a cradle-to-cradle approach where waste is seen as a valuable resource.

Biodiversity Conservation: Biodiversity refers to the variety of plants, animals, and ecosystems on Earth. Protecting and conserving biodiversity is essential for maintaining ecosystem services, such as clean air, water, and soil, as well as for sustaining food production and supporting human well-being.

Sustainable Agriculture: Sustainable agriculture practices prioritize environmental stewardship, social responsibility, and economic viability. This includes organic farming, agroforestry, regenerative agriculture, and reducing the use of synthetic chemicals and genetically modified organisms.

Waste Management: Effective waste management involves reducing waste generation, promoting recycling and composting, and adopting innovative techniques for waste treatment and disposal. It aims to minimize the environmental and health impacts of waste and move towards a circular approach.

Social Equity: Sustainability is not just about the environment; it also encompasses social equity and justice. This involves ensuring fair access to resources, addressing poverty, promoting gender equality, and fostering inclusive and diverse societies.

Sustainable Urbanization: As the world becomes increasingly urbanized, sustainable urban planning and development are crucial. This includes designing energy-efficient buildings, creating green spaces, improving public transportation, and promoting compact and walkable communities.

These are just a few important topics within the broad field of sustainability. Addressing these issues requires collaboration, innovation, and collective action from individuals, businesses, governments, and organizations to create a more sustainable and resilient future

 Transportation is a significant contributor to greenhouse gas emissions. Promoting sustainable transportation options such as public transit, cycling, walking, and electric vehicles can help reduce pollution and congestion while improving air quality and public health.

Climate Change and its consequences

Climate change is caused by human activities, particularly the burning of fossil fuels, releasing greenhouse gases that trap heat and cause temperature rise with consequential impacts.

Consequences of climate change

Rising temperatures: Global average temperatures have been increasing, resulting in heatwaves and heat-related illnesses. High temperatures also contribute to the melting of glaciers and polar ice caps, leading to rising sea levels.

Sea-level rise: As temperatures increase, ice sheets and glaciers melt, causing sea levels to rise. Rising sea levels pose a significant threat to coastal communities, increasing the risk of coastal erosion, flooding, and the loss of habitat for plants and animals.

Extreme weather events: Climate change intensifies extreme weather events such as hurricanes, droughts, wildfires, and heavy rainfall. These events can cause significant damage to infrastructure, agriculture, and ecosystems, and result in the displacement of communities.

Changes in precipitation patterns: Climate change alters rainfall patterns, leading to more frequent and severe droughts in some regions and increased precipitation in others. This affects water availability, agricultural productivity, and can lead to water scarcity and conflicts.

Ecosystem disruption: Climate change impacts ecosystems, leading to shifts in habitats, species extinction, disruption of food chains, and loss of biodiversity. Coral reefs, for example, are highly vulnerable to rising sea temperatures, causing widespread bleaching events and damaging marine ecosystems.

Health impacts: Climate change exacerbates health risks, including heat-related illnesses, respiratory problems due to poor air quality, the spread of vector-borne diseases, and mental health issues caused by displacement and trauma.

Possible solutions and recommendations (climate change)

Transition to renewables, increase energy efficiency, promote electric vehicles, and phase out fossil fuels to mitigate greenhouse gas emissions.

Afforestation and reforestation: Planting trees and restoring forests can help absorb CO_2 from the atmosphere and mitigate climate change. Protecting existing forests is also vital, as they act as carbon sinks and support biodiversity.

Promote energy efficiency in buildings, industries, and transportation to reduce energy consumption and associated emissions.

Adopting sustainable agricultural practices like organic farming and agroforestry reduces emissions and improves resilience to climate change.

Build resilience to climate change by enhancing infrastructure, implementing early warning systems, protecting coastlines, and implementing climate-smart policies.

International cooperation: Climate change is a global issue that requires international cooperation and collective action. Collaboration between countries, through initiatives like the Paris Agreement, is crucial for setting emission reduction targets, sharing knowledge, and providing financial and technological support to developing nations. Addressing climate change necessitates raising awareness, educating communities, and engaging policymakers, businesses, and individuals in sustainable practices.

Renewable Energy

Renewable energy refers to energy derived from sources that are naturally replenished and have a minimal impact on the environment. These sources include solar power, wind power, hydroelectric power, geothermal energy, and biomass. The use of renewable energy is essential for mitigating climate change, reducing greenhouse gas emissions, and achieving a sustainable energy future.

Impacts of not using Renewable Energy

Climate change: The primary impact of not using renewable energy is the continued reliance on fossil fuels, which leads to the release of greenhouse gases into the atmosphere. This contributes to climate change, resulting in rising global temperatures, extreme weather events, sea-level rise, and other adverse environmental consequences.

Air pollution: Burning fossil fuels for energy production releases pollutants such as sulphur dioxide, nitrogen oxides, and particulate matter, leading to air pollution. This pollution is harmful to human health, causing respiratory problems, cardiovascular diseases, and other ailments.

Resource depletion: Fossil fuels are finite resources that will eventually be depleted. As their availability decreases, the cost of extraction and production increases, leading to economic challenges and geopolitical tensions.

Environmental degradation: Extracting and processing fossil fuels often involves destructive practices such as mining and drilling, which result in habitat destruction, water pollution, and ecosystem degradation.

Renewable energy, on the other hand, has minimal environmental impacts, with technologies like solar panels and wind turbines having a smaller ecological footprint.

Possible solutions and recommendations (Renewable Energy)

Increase renewable energy deployment: Governments and policymakers should promote the widespread adoption of renewable energy technologies. This includes incentivizing renewable energy investments, establishing supportive policies and regulations, and facilitating the integration of renewable energy into existing energy systems.

Transition to clean transportation: Promoting electric vehicles (EVs) and expanding charging infrastructure reduces transportation sector emissions and encourages renewable energy adoption.

Enhance research and development: Investing in research and development is crucial for advancing renewable energy technologies, improving their efficiency, and reducing costs. Governments, research institutions, and private companies should collaborate to drive innovation in the renewable energy sector.

Energy storage and grid integration:

Developing efficient energy storage solutions, such as batteries, allows for better integration of intermittent renewable energy sources into the grid. This ensures a reliable and consistent supply of electricity, even during periods of low renewable energy generation.

Promote energy efficiency: Energy efficiency measures reduce energy consumption and the overall demand for energy. By implementing energy-efficient practices in buildings, industries, and appliances, the need for energy generation decreases, easing the transition to renewable energy sources.

Educate and raise awareness: Public education and awareness campaigns play a vital role in promoting the benefits of renewable energy and encouraging individuals, communities, and businesses to embrace sustainable energy practices. Informing the public about the impacts of climate change and the advantages of renewable energy can drive behavioural change and support for renewable energy initiatives.

By prioritizing the development and use of renewable energy, we can significantly reduce greenhouse gas emissions, mitigate climate change, improve air quality, and promote sustainable development. A comprehensive approach that combines policy support, technological advancements, and public engagement is crucial for a successful transition to a renewable energy future.

Resource Conservation

Resource conservation involves sustainable management and efficient use of natural resources, reducing waste, preserving ecosystems, and ensuring availability for future generations. Neglecting it harms the environment, society, and the economy, jeopardizing long-term sustainability, biodiversity, and well-being.

Impacts of not practicing Resource Conservation

Environmental degradation: The extraction, processing, and consumption of natural resources often result in environmental

degradation. Deforestation, habitat destruction, soil erosion, water pollution, and loss of biodiversity are some of the consequences of unsustainable resource exploitation.

Depletion of finite resources: Many natural resources, such as fossil fuels and minerals, are finite and non-renewable. Overconsumption and wasteful practices lead to resource depletion, increasing the cost and scarcity of essential materials.

Energy consumption and greenhouse gas emissions: Extracting, processing, and transporting resources require energy, often sourced from fossil fuels. Increased energy consumption contributes to greenhouse gas emissions and exacerbates climate change.

Waste generation and landfill burden: Insufficient resource conservation leads to high levels of waste generation. This places a burden on landfills, increases pollution risks, and results in the loss of valuable materials that could be recycled or reused.

Socioeconomic implications: Unsustainable resource management causes socioeconomic issues like price volatility, instability, conflicts, and impacts communities relying on natural resources.

Possible solutions and recommendation for resource conservation

 Encourage responsible consumption patterns by promoting sustainable and eco-friendly products. Implement policies and initiatives that support sustainable production practices, such as eco-design, resource-efficient manufacturing, and waste reduction measures.

Recycling and waste management: Establish comprehensive recycling and waste management systems to minimize the amount of waste sent to landfills. Promote recycling programs, incentivize waste reduction, and educate the public about proper waste disposal practices.

Circular economy approaches: Adopt a circular economy model that aims to keep resources in use for as long as possible. This involves designing products for durability, repairability, and recyclability, as well as promoting the reuse and repurposing of materials.

Conservation and restoration of ecosystems: Preserving habitats and ecosystems is vital for biodiversity. Prevent deforestation, promote reforestation, and protect vulnerable ecosystems.

Efficient use of water resources: Implement water conservation strategies in agriculture, industry, and households. Encourage the use of water-saving technologies, promote responsible water use practices, and invest in water-efficient irrigation systems.

Renewable and clean energy transition: Transition to renewable energy to reduce fossil fuel dependency and promote clean energy adoption. Effective resource conservation is essential for sustainability and requires collaboration across sectors.

Circular Economy

The circular economy maximizes resource efficiency, minimizes waste, and promotes product reuse, recycling, and redesign for positive environmental, social, and economic outcomes.

Impacts of implementing a circular economy

Resource conservation: Circular economy conserves resources by promoting reuse, recycling, and repurposing. It reduces extraction, waste, and environmental degradation, ensuring sustainable resource management for a greener future.

Waste reduction: Circular economy minimizes waste through durable, repairable, recyclable design. Recycling cuts landfill waste, promotes sustainable resource usage. It lowers energy consumption, carbon footprint, and emissions through renewable energy and efficient practices in extraction, production, and waste management.

The circular economy promotes economic growth and job creation through recycling, repair, remanufacturing, and eco-design. It fosters innovation, sustainable technology investment, and competitiveness. By prioritizing durable products, it satisfies customers, promotes sustainability, and fosters sustainable supply chains through collaboration and responsible sourcing.

In conclusion, the failure to adopt a circular economy approach results in increased waste, resource depletion, environmental degradation, economic inefficiency, and missed opportunities for job creation and social benefits. Embracing the circular economy is crucial for a sustainable future and the well-being of both the planet and its inhabitants.

Possible recommendations for implementing Circular Economy Design for circularity: Adopt eco-design principles that prioritize product durability, reparability, and recyclability while encourage the use of renewable and recyclable materials, and design products with disassembly and recycling in mind.

Promote reuse and sharing: Promote sharing economy: Rent, buy second-hand, and share resources through platforms for reusing products and materials.

Efficient recycling requires robust infrastructure to recover materials from end-of-life products, while raising public awareness and promoting participation in recycling programs.

Embrace remanufacturing and refurbishment: Support remanufacturing industries that restore used products to a like-new condition, extending their lifespan and reducing waste. Provide incentives for refurbishment and repair services.

Educate and raise awareness Promote circular economy: Educate stakeholders, implement supportive policies, foster collaboration, and drive innovation for a sustainable future, minimizing waste and maximizing economic and environmental benefits.

Biodiversity Conservation

Biodiversity conservation protects Earth's variety of life, including ecosystems, species, and genetic diversity. It maintains ecosystem balance, provides services, and sustains human well-being with ecological, environmental, social, and economic benefits.

Impacts of Biodiversity Conservation

Biodiversity supports ecosystem stability by ensuring the functioning of ecological processes and maintaining productivity through conservation efforts.

Conserving biodiverse ecosystems, like forests, wetlands, and oceans, helps regulate the climate and mitigate climate change impacts by storing carbon dioxide.

Provision of ecosystem services: Biodiversity conservation ensures the continued provision of vital ecosystem services, such as clean air and water, fertile soil, and natural resources. These services are essential for human well-being, supporting agriculture, fisheries, medicine, and tourism, among other industries.

Genetic resources and future innovations: Biodiversity is a source of genetic diversity, which provides the foundation for the development of new medicines, crops, and technologies. Conserving diverse species and their genetic resources preserves potential future discoveries and innovations that can benefit society.

Cultural and spiritual values: Biodiversity is vital to cultural and spiritual practices of communities worldwide. Indigenous peoples and local communities depend on it for livelihoods, traditions, and spiritual well-being. Conservation safeguards cultural diversity and protects indigenous rights.

Biodiversity-rich areas attract tourists interested in experiencing unique ecosystems and wildlife. Conservation efforts can support the development of sustainable ecotourism, generating economic benefits for local communities and contributing to the conservation of biodiversity.

Resilience to environmental changes:

Conserving biodiversity strengthen ecosystem and species resilience to environmental changes. Amid habitat loss, pollution, and climate change threats, preservation enables adaptation and survival.

Preservation of ecosystem beauty and inspiration:

Biodiversity encompasses a wide range of captivating and awe-inspiring species and habitats. Conserving biodiversity preserves the beauty of natural landscapes and provides inspiration for art, culture, and human well-being.

Possible solutions and recommendations for Biodiversity Conservation

Protected areas and habitat preservation: Establish and effectively manage protected areas, including national parks, reserves, and wildlife sanctuaries. Protecting critical habitats is essential for preserving biodiversity and providing safe haven for endangered species.

Sustainable land and resource management: Promote sustainable land-use practices that prioritize biodiversity conservation, such as sustainable agriculture, forestry, and fisheries. Implement responsible resource extraction methods that minimize habitat destruction and maintain ecosystem integrity.

Combatting illegal wildlife trade requires strengthening law enforcement, promoting international cooperation, raising awareness, and reducing the demand for wildlife products

Raise public awareness and encourage sustainable choices to conserve biodiversity, while fostering collaboration and international cooperation for effective conservation initiatives and funding.

Support local communities and indigenous people:
Involve local communities and indigenous peoples in biodiversity conservation efforts, respecting their traditional knowledge and rights. Provide support for sustainable livelihoods that are compatible with biodiversity conservation. Restoration and reforestation: Implement programs for habitat restoration and reforestation to recover degraded ecosystems and enhance biodiversity.

Support initiatives that promote native plant species and restore connectivity between fragmented habitats.

Incorporate biodiversity conservation into development planning and prioritize sustainable practices to protect ecosystems and biodiversity. Address climate change impacts by reducing emissions and supporting adaptive strategies for species and ecosystems. Biodiversity conservation is essential for a sustainable future, involving scientific knowledge, policy support, community engagement, and sustainable practices to protect and restore ecosystems and their services.

Sustainable Agriculture

Sustainable agriculture refers to the practice of cultivating food, fibre, and other agricultural products in a manner that conserves natural resources, minimizes environmental impacts, and promotes the long-term viability of farming systems. It aims to balance economic profitability, social equity, and environmental stewardship. Sustainable agriculture has significant impacts on various aspects of society, the environment, and the economy. If sustainable agriculture practices are not adopted, it can lead to detrimental consequences.

Impacts of not using sustainable agriculture practices

Soil degradation: Unsustainable agricultural practices, such as excessive use of synthetic fertilizers, pesticides, and intensive tillage, can lead to soil degradation. Soil erosion, nutrient depletion, and loss of soil organic matter can reduce soil fertility, affecting crop productivity and long-term agricultural sustainability.

 Intensive agricultural practices often involve the use of chemical inputs that can leach into water bodies, leading to water pollution. Runoff from fields carrying pesticides and fertilizers can contaminate surface and groundwater, affecting aquatic ecosystems and human health. Additionally, unsustainable irrigation practices can deplete water resources, leading to water scarcity.

Biodiversity loss: Conventional agriculture's habitat destruction for expanding farmland leads to biodiversity loss, disrupting ecosystems, pollination services, and pest control.

Greenhouse gas emissions: Unsustainable agricultural practices, such as the use of synthetic fertilizers and improper management of livestock waste, can contribute to greenhouse gas emissions. Nitrous oxide emissions from synthetic fertilizers and methane emissions from livestock contribute to climate change and global warming.

Public health impacts: Overreliance on chemical inputs in agriculture jeopardizes human health through pesticide residues in food and antibiotic resistance in livestock farming.

Loss of rural livelihoods: Unsustainable agricultural practices result in the loss of rural livelihoods, as small-scale farmers are displaced and economic viability declines.

Unsustainable resource use in conventional agriculture jeopardizes long-term sustainability by depleting resources and emitting carbon emissions.

Possible solutions and recommendations for Sustainable Agriculture

Organic farming: Promote and support organic farming practices that eliminate the use of synthetic chemicals and prioritize soil health, biodiversity conservation, and sustainable pest management techniques.

Agroforestry: Promote agroforestry systems that combine trees with crops or livestock. Agroforestry provides multiple benefits, including improved soil fertility, biodiversity conservation, carbon sequestration, and diversified income sources for farmers.

Water conservation and efficient irrigation: Encourage the use of efficient irrigation systems, such as drip irrigation and precision irrigation, to minimize water waste. Implement water management strategies that promote water conservation, including rainwater harvesting and water recycling.

Integrated pest management (IPM): Advocate for the use of IPM practices that focus on biological control, cultural practices, and targeted use of pesticides as a last resort. IPM reduces pesticide use, protects beneficial insects, and promotes ecosystem balance.

Conservation agriculture: Encourage the adoption of conservation agriculture techniques, such as minimal tillage, cover cropping, and crop rotation. These practices help preserve soil structure, enhance water retention, reduce erosion, and promote soil health.

Sustainable livestock management: Promote sustainable livestock farming practices, including rotational grazing, improved waste management systems, and reduced use of antibiotics. These practices reduce greenhouse gas emissions, protect water quality, and enhance animal welfare.

Agroecology and permaculture: Support agroecological and permaculture approaches that integrate ecological principles into farming systems. These approaches emphasize biodiversity, soil health, and ecological interactions to promote sustainable and resilient agricultural systems.

Support small-scale farmers: Provide technical support, access to markets, and financial incentives to small-scale farmers practicing sustainable agriculture. Empower local communities and promote equitable access to resources and markets.

Education and knowledge sharing: Promote education and awareness programs to disseminate knowledge about sustainable agriculture practices among farmers, consumers, and policymakers. Encourage research and innovation to develop and implement sustainable agricultural technologies and practices.

Adopting sustainable agriculture practices mitigates environmental impacts, preserves resources, protects biodiversity, ensures food security, and promotes long-term agricultural viability through regenerative and holistic approaches.

Waste Management

Waste management refers to the collection, transportation, disposal, and recycling of waste materials in a manner that minimizes environmental impacts, protects public health, and promotes resource efficiency. Proper waste management is crucial to prevent adverse consequences that can occur if waste is not handled correctly. These impacts can be seen in various aspects of the environment, public health, and sustainability.

Impacts of Improper Waste Management

Environmental pollution: When waste is not managed properly, it can lead to environmental pollution. Dumping waste in open areas, water bodies, or improper landfills can contaminate soil, water and air. Hazardous substances in waste can leach into the soil and water, causing pollution and posing risks to ecosystems and wildlife.

Health hazards: Improper waste management can pose significant risks to public health. Accumulation of waste can attract pests, such as rodents and insects, which can spread diseases. Exposure to toxic chemicals and pathogens in waste can lead to respiratory problems, gastrointestinal illnesses, skin infections, and other health issues.

Soil and water contamination: Improper disposal of waste can contaminate soil and water resources. Landfills lacking proper liners and leachate management systems can release pollutants into the surrounding soil and groundwater, affecting water quality and harming plant and animal life.

Air pollution: Open burning of waste, a common practice in some areas, releases harmful pollutants into the air, including toxic gases, particulate matter, and greenhouse gases. These emissions contribute to air pollution and can have detrimental effects on human health and the environment.

Resource depletion: Improper waste management results in the loss of valuable resources, depleting natural resources and increasing the demand for new materials. Recycling and reusing waste can prevent this loss.

Greenhouse gas emissions: Organic waste, such as food waste and yard waste, that ends up in landfills produces methane, a potent greenhouse gas. Methane contributes to climate change and global warming. Improper waste management practices contribute to unnecessary greenhouse gas emissions.

Aesthetics and quality of life: Improper waste management lowers community well-being and tourism potential by creating unsightly and unhygienic conditions in public spaces, streets, and water bodies, reducing overall quality of life for residents.

Waste reduction and recycling: Emphasize waste reduction at the source through practices such as promoting reusable products,

composting organic waste, and implementing recycling programs. Encourage recycling of materials like paper, plastic, glass, and metal to reduce waste sent to landfills.

Waste segregation: Implement waste segregation at the point of generation to separate recyclable materials from non-recyclable waste. Properly labelled recycling bins can facilitate segregation and enable efficient recycling processes.

Composting: Encourage composting of organic waste, such as food scraps and yard trimmings, to divert these materials from landfills.

Composting creates nutrient-rich compost that can be used for soil enrichment in gardens and agriculture.

Waste-to-energy systems: Implement waste-to-energy technologies, such as anaerobic digestion or incineration with energy recovery, to convert non-recyclable waste into renewable energy sources, reducing reliance on fossil fuels.

Proper landfill management: Implement modern landfill management practices, including the use of impermeable liners, leachate collection systems, and methane capture. This minimizes environmental contamination and harnesses methane gas for energy generation.

Public awareness and education: Conduct public awareness campaigns to educate individuals about the importance of proper waste management practices. Encourage responsible waste disposal, segregation, and recycling habits.

Extended producer responsibility (EPR): Implement EPR policies that hold manufacturers responsible for the entire lifecycle of their products, including proper waste management and recycling. This incentivizes sustainable product design and reduces waste generation.

Collaboration and partnerships: Foster collaboration among government agencies, waste management companies, businesses, and communities to develop integrated waste management plans, infrastructure, and facilities. Public-private partnerships can help improve waste management practices.

Technological advancements: Invest in research and development of innovative waste management technologies, such as advanced sorting and recycling systems, waste treatment technologies, and waste tracking systems, to improve efficiency and reduce environmental impacts.

Implementing effective waste management practices is essential for mitigating the environmental, health, and sustainability impacts associated with improper waste handling. It requires a comprehensive approach that involves waste reduction, recycling, proper disposal, and resource recovery to create a more sustainable and circular economy.

Waste segregation is crucial in waste management, categorizing waste into wet (organic) and dry (non-biodegradable) types. This enables efficient treatment and recycling, promoting effective waste management processes.

Wet Waste (Organic Waste): Wet waste includes biodegradable materials like food scraps, peels, tea leaves, and garden waste that decompose naturally. Mixing wet waste with dry waste in landfills produces methane gas, contributing to greenhouse gas emissions and environmental pollution.

Benefits of segregating wet waste:

Composting: Segregated wet waste can be used for composting. Composting is a natural process that converts organic waste into nutrient-rich compost, which can be used as a natural fertilizer for gardens, parks, and agricultural fields.

Dry Waste (Non-biodegradable Waste): Dry waste refers to non-biodegradable materials such as plastic, glass, metal, paper, cardboard, electronic waste, and other recyclable materials. These

items do not decompose naturally and can persist in the environment for a long time, causing pollution and resource depletion if not properly managed.

Benefits of segregating dry waste:

Recycling: Segregated dry waste can be sent for recycling. Recycling involves the conversion of waste materials into new products, reducing the need for virgin materials, conserving resources, and minimizing environmental impacts.

Resource conservation: By segregating dry waste, valuable materials can be recovered and reused, reducing the extraction of raw materials and conserving natural resources.

Waste-to-energy: Certain types of dry waste, such as non-recyclable plastics, can be utilized in waste-to-energy facilities, where they are converted into energy sources like electricity or heat through processes like incineration with energy recovery.

Waste segregation methods and recommendations:

Separate collection bins: Provide separate collection bins or containers for wet and dry waste in households, offices, public spaces, and other areas to encourage proper segregation at the source.

Clear labelling: Clearly label the bins with instructions and visual aids to help individuals differentiate between wet and dry waste.

Public awareness campaigns: Conduct educational programs, workshops, and awareness campaigns to inform the public about the importance of segregating waste and the benefits it offers.

 Train waste management personnel and engage communities in waste segregation initiatives to ensure effective implementation and participation.

 Implement regulations and monitoring systems to enforce proper waste segregation practices, and impose penalties for non-compliance if necessary.

 Establish appropriate waste management infrastructure, including waste collection systems, recycling facilities, and composting units, to support the segregation and processing of waste.

Segregating wet and dry waste at the source improves waste management by enabling efficient processing, resource recovery, and environmental sustainability.

Social Equity

Social equity refers to the concept of fairness, justice, and equal opportunities in society. It focuses on ensuring that all individuals have access to basic needs, resources, and opportunities regardless of their background, socioeconomic status, race, gender, or other factors. When social equity is not put in place properly, it can lead to various negative impacts on individuals, communities, and society as a whole.

Impacts of not promoting social equity

Inequality and marginalization: Without social equity, marginalized groups, such as low-income individuals, minorities, and disadvantaged communities, may face discrimination, limited access to resources, and exclusion from decision-making processes. This can perpetuate social and economic disparities, leading to increased poverty, unemployment, and social unrest.

Limited social mobility: Inequitable systems can restrict social mobility, making it difficult for individuals to break free from intergenerational poverty or discrimination. This can hinder personal growth, educational opportunities, and upward mobility, creating barriers to achieving a better quality of life.

Health disparities: Lack of social equity can result in unequal access to healthcare services, leading to health disparities. Marginalized communities may experience higher rates of diseases, limited healthcare resources, and inadequate healthcare coverage, exacerbating health inequalities.

Education gaps: Inequities in education systems can create disparities in academic achievement and opportunities. Students from marginalized backgrounds may have limited access to quality education, resulting in lower educational attainment, reduced employment prospects, and perpetuation of socioeconomic inequalities.

Social cohesion and stability: Inequity can erode social cohesion and trust within communities. When individuals feel marginalized or excluded, it can lead to social unrest, conflicts, and a breakdown of social bonds, hindering overall societal development and stability.

Possible solutions and recommendations for promoting social equity

Ensure equitable access to quality education, healthcare, housing, employment, and essential services for all individuals, regardless of socioeconomic or demographic factors.

Address systemic biases, promote diversity and inclusion, and ensure equitable outcomes by identifying and addressing discriminatory practices within institutions and systems

Income and wealth redistribution: Implement policies that aim to reduce income and wealth disparities through progressive taxation, social safety nets, and targeted social welfare programs to uplift disadvantaged individuals & communities.

Invest in education and skills development to provide equal opportunities for personal and professional growth.

Community engagement and participation: Foster community engagement, involvement, and empowerment to ensure marginalized groups have a voice in decision-making and community-led initiatives.

Establish robust social safety nets, including healthcare, unemployment benefits, and assistance programs, to prevent poverty and support individuals during challenging times.

Implement and enforce anti-discrimination laws and policies, promoting diversity, inclusivity, and equality across all societal domains.

Sustainable Transportation

Sustainable transportation refers to the use of transportation systems and modes that minimize environmental impacts, promote energy efficiency, and prioritize social and economic equity. When sustainable transportation practices are not implemented, it can lead to various negative impacts on the environment, public health, and the economy.

Key impacts of not using sustainable transportation

Environmental degradation: Conventional transportation's reliance on fossil fuels contributes to greenhouse gas emissions, air pollution, climate change, and environmental degradation, affecting ecosystems and human health.

Public health issues: Traditional transportation systems, including private cars and diesel-powered vehicles, contribute to air pollution, affecting both physical and mental health.

Congestion and inefficiency: Overreliance on personal vehicles cause traffic congestion, wasted time, increased fuel consumption, emissions, strained infrastructure, and limited economic growth potential.

Social inequality: Limited sustainable transportation options exacerbate social inequality by hindering access to essential services, jobs, and education, particularly for low-income communities.

Economic costs: Unsustainable transportation practices incur substantial economic costs, including road maintenance, congestion, healthcare expenses, and vulnerability to fossil fuel price fluctuations and supply disruptions.

over private vehicles.

Several solutions and recommendations for sustainable transportation

Enhance public transportation: Invest in efficient and reliable public transportation systems, including buses, trains, and light rail systems. Improve accessibility, affordability, and frequency of service to encourage more people to choose public transportation

Active transportation infrastructure: Develop and expand infrastructure for walking, cycling, and other non-motorized modes of transportation. Promote pedestrian-friendly cities, build dedicated bicycle lanes, and implement bike-sharing programs to encourage active commuting.

Electrification and alternative fuels: Transition to electric vehicles (EVs) and promote the development of charging infrastructure. Support the adoption of alternative fuels, such as hydrogen and biofuels, to reduce carbon emissions and   dependence on fossil fuels.

Land-use planning: Implement smart urban planning strategies that promote mixed-use development, reducing the need for long-distance commuting. Create walkable neighbourhoods, with amenities within proximity, to encourage shorter trips and reduce reliance on cars.

Carpooling and ridesharing: Encourage carpooling and ridesharing programs to reduce the number of single-occupancy vehicles on the road. Promote the use of ride-hailing services that utilize electric or hybrid vehicles.

Telecommuting and flexible work arrangements: Encourage employers to adopt telecommuting and flexible work schedules, reducing the need for daily commuting and alleviating peak-hour congestion.

Telecommuting, also known as remote work or work-from-home arrangements, refers to the practice of employees working from a location outside of their traditional workplace, usually their homes. Implementing telecommuting and flexible work arrangements can have various positive impacts on individuals, businesses, and the environment. Here are the impacts and benefits of such arrangements:

Reduced commuting and transportation emissions: One of the significant benefits of telecommuting is the reduction in commuting trips. By working from home, employees eliminate or reduce their daily commutes, resulting in lower transportation emissions. This reduction in carbon emissions contributes to mitigating climate change and improving air quality.

Increased productivity and job satisfaction: Studies have shown that employees who telecommute experience higher levels of productivity and job satisfaction. By eliminating the stress and time spent on commuting, employees can focus more on their work tasks, resulting in improved efficiency and overall job satisfaction.

Improved work-life balance: Telecommuting provides employees with the flexibility to better manage their personal and professional lives. They can save time on commuting, have more control over their work schedules, and allocate time for personal responsibilities. This balance can lead to reduced stress levels, increased well-being, and better mental health.

Cost savings: Telecommuting can result in cost savings for both employees and employers. Employees can save money on commuting expenses, such as fuel, parking fees, or public transportation fares. Employers can reduce overhead costs associated with maintaining office space and facilities.

Enhanced employee retention and recruitment: Offering telecommuting options can be an attractive perk for employees, leading to improved employee retention rates. It can also broaden the pool of potential candidates during the recruitment process, as location constraints are minimized, allowing businesses to access a larger talent pool.

Business continuity and resilience: Telecommuting provides a solution for maintaining business operations during unforeseen circumstances or disruptions, such as natural disasters, pandemics, or transportation strikes. It enables businesses to continue functioning and serving clients even when physical office spaces are inaccessible.

Reduced traffic congestion and infrastructure strain: By reducing the number of commuters on the roads, telecommuting can alleviate traffic congestion, particularly during peak hours. This not only improves traffic flow but also reduces the strain on transportation infrastructure, resulting in smoother mobility for those who do need to travel.

To effectively implement telecommuting and flexible work arrangements, the following recommendations can be considered:

Establish clear policies and guidelines: Develop comprehensive policies and guidelines that outline telecommuting eligibility, expectations, communication protocols, and performance evaluation criteria. Ensure that employees understand the requirements and responsibilities associated with remote work.

Provide necessary technology and support: Equip employees with the necessary technology, such as laptops, secure network access, and collaboration tools, to facilitate remote work. Offer technical support to address any issues that may arise during telecommuting.

Maintain effective communication: Foster regular and open communication channels among team members and between employees and managers. Utilize communication tools like video conferencing, instant messaging, and project management platforms to ensure effective collaboration and information sharing.

Set performance goals and metrics: Establish clear performance goals and metrics to ensure accountability and productivity in a **remote work environment**. Regularly assess and evaluate the performance of remote employees based on agreed-upon objectives and outcomes.

Encourage social interaction and team building: Facilitate virtual team building activities, **online meetings**, and social gatherings to maintain team cohesion and foster a sense of belonging among

remote employees. This helps to mitigate feelings of isolation and promote collaboration.

Continuously evaluate and improve: Regularly review the telecommuting program to identify areas for improvement and address any challenges or concerns that arise. Seek feedback from employees to better understand their needs and make necessary adjustments to optimize the effectiveness of remote work arrangements.

By embracing telecommuting and flexible work arrangements, businesses can create a more sustainable work environment, improve employee well-being and satisfaction, reduce environmental impacts, and enhance operational resilience. It is essential for organizations to adapt to changing work trends and leverage technology to facilitate remote work effectively.

Promote education, awareness, and behaviour change to raise public understanding of the environmental and health impacts of transportation choices, encouraging sustainable transportation options through campaigns, incentives, and information sharing.

Sustainable transportation practices mitigate environmental damage, improve public health, reduce congestion, promote social equity, and foster economic resilience, necessitating collaborative efforts to invest in infrastructure, promote behaviour change, and create a transportation system that meets needs while preserving the planet for future generations.

Sustainable Urbanization

Sustainable urbanization entails developing cities that meet current needs while safeguarding future generations' abilities to do the same. It encompasses environmentally friendly, socially inclusive, and economically viable cities. Ignoring sustainable urbanization can result in various negative consequences. Let's explore the impacts of unsustainable urbanization and potential solutions.

Impacts of unsustainable Urbanization

Environmental degradation: unsustainable urbanization can lead to environmental degradation through increased pollution, deforestation, loss of biodiversity, and inefficient use of resources. It can contribute to air and water pollution, climate change, and the destruction of natural habitats.

Increased energy consumption: Poorly planned urbanization can result in increased energy consumption due to the high demand for heating, cooling, and transportation. This reliance on fossil fuels leads to greenhouse gas emissions, contributing to climate change.

Traffic congestion and reduced mobility: Unplanned urbanization often results in increased traffic congestion, longer commuting times, and reduced mobility. This leads to wasted time, increased fuel consumption, and air pollution. It also negatively affects economic productivity and quality of life for urban residents.

Inadequate infrastructure: Rapid and unplanned urbanization can strain existing infrastructure, including transportation, water supply, sanitation, and waste management systems. Inadequate infrastructure hinders the provision of essential services and negatively impacts the quality of life for urban residents.

Social inequality: Unsustainable urbanization can exacerbate social inequality. Informal settlements, slums, and inadequate housing become prevalent in cities, leading to poor living conditions and limited access to basic services such as education, healthcare, and clean water. This further widens the gap between the rich and the poor.

Solutions and recommendations for sustainable Urbanization

Integrated urban planning: Develop comprehensive urban planning strategies that consider social, economic, and environmental aspects. Foster compact and mixed-use urban development, prioritizing public transportation, walkability, and bike-friendly infrastructure. Promote the use of green spaces, parks, and urban agriculture.

Efficient resource management: Implement sustainable practices for resource management, such as energy-efficient buildings, renewable energy integration, water conservation measures, and waste management systems that prioritize recycling and waste reduction.

 Ensure access to affordable and adequate housing for all urban residents. Promote social housing programs, encourage mixed-income neighbourhoods, and enforce regulations to prevent informal settlements and slum proliferation.

 Invest in efficient and accessible public transportation systems, including buses, trams, subways, and light rail. Develop integrated transportation networks that prioritize public transit, pedestrian-friendly infrastructure, and cycling lanes to reduce reliance on private vehicles.

 Preserve and expand urban green spaces, including parks, gardens, and natural areas. Create protected areas and wildlife corridors to support biodiversity conservation within cities.

 Foster community engagement and participation in urban planning processes. Involve residents, local organizations, and stakeholders in decision-making to ensure their needs and concerns are considered.

Education and awareness: Promote public education and awareness campaigns to inform residents about sustainable urban living, waste reduction, energy conservation, and the benefits of sustainable practices. Encourage behaviour change and responsible consumption patterns.

Collaborative governance: Foster collaboration between government authorities, private sector entities, civil society organizations, and academia to implement sustainable urbanization practices. Establish partnerships and share knowledge and best practices.

By adopting sustainable urbanization principles and implementing these solutions, cities can create liveable, resilient, and inclusive urban environments that improve the quality of life for residents, protect the environment, and support long-term social and economic development.

Carbon (Co2) footprint: Factory example

Calculating carbon footprint involves quantifying the total greenhouse gas emissions, particularly carbon dioxide (CO_2), resulting from an individual, organization, or activity.

Some general steps to calculate CO2 footprint & suggestions to reduce carbon footprint

Identify Scope: Determine the scope of the assessment by specifying the boundaries of the analysis, such as direct emissions from owned or controlled sources (Scope 1), indirect emissions from purchased energy (Scope 2), and other indirect emissions from the value chain (Scope 3).

Gather Data: Collect data on energy consumption, fuel usage, transportation, waste generation, and other relevant activities within the defined scope.

Convert Data: Convert the collected data into CO2 equivalents using emission factors specific to each emission source. Emission factors are typically available from recognized databases or industry standards.

Calculate Emissions: Multiply the data from each emission source by its corresponding emission factor to calculate CO2 emissions.

Summarize Results: Add up all the calculated CO2 emissions to obtain the total carbon footprint. You can leverage free or paid Carbon calculators available across the internet.

Suggestions to reduce carbon footprint:

Energy Efficiency: Implement energy-efficient technologies and practices, including efficient machinery, lighting, insulation, and heating/cooling systems.

Renewable Energy: Install renewable energy systems, such as solar panels or wind turbines, to replace or supplement traditional energy sources.

Waste Management: Optimize waste management processes, prioritize recycling and waste reduction, and consider implementing waste-to-energy solutions.

Supply Chain Optimization: Collaborate with suppliers to promote sustainable practices, reduce emissions in the supply chain, and minimize transportation-related emissions.

Employee Engagement: Educate and involve employees in sustainability initiatives, encouraging them to adopt energy-saving habits and contribute to emission reduction efforts.

Process Optimization: Identify and optimize energy-intensive processes, reducing energy consumption and associated emissions without compromising product quality.

Continuous Improvement: Regularly monitor and analyse energy usage, emissions, and environmental performance to identify areas for improvement and set targets for reduction.

By implementing these measures and considering site-specific opportunities, factories/Industries can significantly reduce their carbon footprint and contribute to a more sustainable future.

End Note (The Beginning)

A good carbon footprint percentage is relative and depends on various factors, including the context, industry, and available resources. However, the general aim is to reduce carbon footprint as much as possible to mitigate climate change and minimize environmental impact.

The ultimate goal is to achieve net-zero carbon emissions, where the amount of CO_2 emitted is balanced by an equivalent amount of CO_2 removed from the atmosphere through measures like carbon offsets or carbon sequestration.

In terms of specific targets, many organizations and countries have set goals to reduce their carbon footprint. For example, the Paris Agreement, an international climate accord, aims to limit global warming to well below 2 degrees Celsius above pre-industrial levels and pursue efforts to limit the temperature increase to 1.5 degrees Celsius.

To achieve this, countries have committed to reducing their greenhouse gas emissions, including CO_2, to reach net-zero emissions by the second half of the century.

It is important for businesses and individuals to assess their own carbon footprint and set reduction targets based on their specific circumstances. The goal should be to continuously improve and reduce emissions over time, working towards sustainability and a low-carbon future.

Together, let's collaborate and strive towards a future world that is sustainable, where the needs of the present are met without compromising the ability of future generations to meet their own needs.